Baby's Room

To the

BOARD ROOM

A Guide for Working Moms:
How to Transition from Bottle Feeding to Boss Moves!

Baby's Room

To the

BOARD ROOM

*A Guide for Working Moms:
How to Transition from Bottle Feeding to Boss Moves!*

LETITIA CLARK

Halo
PUBLISHING
INTERNATIONAL

Halo Publishing International
8000 W Interstate 10, #600
San Antonio, Texas 78230

First Edition, March 2023
ISBN: 978-1-63765-378-4
Library of Congress Control Number: 2023902524

Halo Publishing International is a self-publishing company that publishes adult fiction and non-fiction, children's literature, self-help, spiritual, and faith-based books. We continually strive to help authors reach their publishing goals and provide many different services that help them do so. We do not publish books that are deemed to be politically, religiously, or socially disrespectful, or books that are sexually provocative, including erotica. Halo reserves the right to refuse publication of any manuscript if it is deemed not to be in line with our principles. Do you have a book idea you would like us to consider publishing? Please visit www.halopublishing.com for more information.

To All the Ladies of Style and Grace

This book is dedicated to my mother, Christella; her mother, my grandmother Elenora; her sisters, my aunts Brenda, Aleta, and Pamela, and my late aunt Linda. To my auntie Sheila and my godmom Sandra; to my mother-in-law, Joanne; and to all the women in my life who have shown me what it means to be a loving mom...while working to make the community and ourselves better.

This book is also dedicated to my paternal grandmother, Marion, who at ninety has a lifetime of stories that include living in the Jim Crow South; raising a family in Orange County, California; and experiencing instances of overt and covert discrimination.

Granny's story, like my mother's and those of the other women in my life, served as examples of how to thrive instead of just survive. Their stories provide inspiration in how to look at big mountains as if they were little molehills, and in how to nevertheless...persist.

To the Three Who Made Me a Mom

Being a mother is a huge part of my identity; it has served as the greatest joy, yet most consuming part, of my entire life. My love for my kids is so immense, and I take the responsibility of their care and well-being seriously. Raising them consistently teaches me about myself and the world around us. They make me better. Carin, Theodore, and Zavier—Mommy loves you three more than you may ever know.

The Village

I also have to show love to my handsome husband, Zach, who supports me in being the best mom, professional, and woman I can be. I love you.

While I'm at it, I would like to send love to everyone in my life who forms the village in raising my kids —my dad, Michael; sisters Candace and Cortni; and brother, Mikey.

To all the people in my life who help with the hard job of mothering—from providing counseling, laughter, advice, or just love—my high school and college friends, my sorority sisters, and the friends I've gained as an adult.

With love, respect, and admiration, I love you all.

Contents

Introduction

I first started writing this book as a single mom to nine-year-old twins, after being divorced for four years, while regaining my sea legs in my career, and after winning a seat in an elected office.

Fast forward, I started writing again after my life completely changed, but the lessons were that much more relevant. The twins had become teenagers. I was a wife again, having married the love of my life. I had won reelection and was serving as mayor. I had gotten pregnant with baby number three and had returned to work after my pregnancy leave. All in the height of a global pandemic.

The lessons I learned as a new mom with twins, and then those taught to me after having another baby fourteen years later as a forty-year-old mom while working full-time, are similar in many aspects. I've learned that, for working moms, there is never enough time, mom guilt is real, America needs better maternity-leave policies, and work-life balance is a fallacy.

I've also learned not to sweat the small stuff, female instinct is valid and valuable, and the woman I was before I had kids is long gone. However, instead of mourning the loss of that woman, I've embraced and celebrated the new woman I have become and the one into whom I continue to evolve.

In fact, one of the greatest lessons that I've learned is that I don't have to separate the woman I am as a mom from the woman I am as a professional—the two can coexist in the same space.

Although I am still very much in the thick of making it work as a working mom, I can confidently say that there is a bright light inside the tunnel, and I don't have to wait until my kids are grown or until I retire to see it.

What This Book Is Not

Before you get your hopes too high, please let me make clear that this book will not show you how to have it all. This book will not transform you into the Supermom who feels and looks great while her kids do the same. This book will not stop you from having moments of frustration, burnout, or feeling like a failure.

What This Book Is

However, this book will (hopefully) help remind you that you're not alone, you're not crazy, and you *will* make it through.

Many of my stories will feel familiar; some, completely foreign. But my hope is that you will connect to just a few of them and realize that being a parent does not diminish what you can bring to your profession. Moreover, I hope that you can learn from some of my experiences and look at being a mom as an *asset, not a liability.* I hope this book helps you maneuver into the true mom boss you are destined to become.

Baby's Room to the BoardRoom is a pocketbook full of tips, tricks, and tools based on real-life experiences that have helped me navigate between the matrices that working moms juggle between. I hope that they will help you too.

Lesson 1

Basic Instinct
—*Trust Your Gut*

Baby's Room

When first learning that I would become a mom, I was pretty freaked out. I grew up with three younger siblings, but besides my interaction with them, I did not have much experience with kids. At twenty-five, I worried about normal new-mom duties, such as breastfeeding and baby safety, but didn't know how to properly change a diaper or where to register for baby gifts. On top of everything, I was becoming the mom of twins, which brought even more concerns. Sleepless nights were fueled by worry, on top of midnight baby-kick sessions. I bought so many books and subscribed to blogs and magazines, and yet my self-teaching only made me more concerned for the health of my soon-to-be-born babies.

I consistently tortured myself with the same questions: Will the twins be healthy? Is the house ready for babies? Will I be able to breastfeed? Do we have everything we need? Will I be a good mom?

A few months into mommyhood and the struggle was real in terms of sleep and balance; however, I noticed that some of those fundamental and pervasive questions seemed less important. My instinct as a mother definitely started to come into play. The babies were doing some things quite naturally on their own, and so was I. A sense of empowerment came over me because the gut feeling and internal voice that I had grown to hear as a woman was stronger *than ever. And while I used to ignore and dismiss that voice, as a mom I was learning to lean in closer and listen more intently.*

When returning to work, I didn't forget the strength and security that my instinct provided while being a new mom. I remembered that feeling and followed it faithfully in my professional life when it was time to ask for a raise, take on new responsibilities, resolve conflicts, or seek professional development. That basic instinct that every woman possesses was illuminated in me as a mom.

BOARDROOM

We often forget the power of our basic instincts. When faced with tough challenges in your professional journey, remember that your ability to lead and succeed will come very naturally if you lean on your basic instinct and intuition.

Resist the urge to doubt yourself, count yourself out, compare yourself to others, or consume too much negative information and feedback. Remember how you survived as a new mom and how the most important things came very naturally. Of course, we all experience struggles in various ways, but start new professional challenges by giving yourself credit for being able to figure things out instinctually.

Lesson 2

Nesting—Envision and Create Space for the Future You

Baby's Room

Planning the baby area or room is not only fun, but it helps you mentally prepare for and manifest the arrival of your child. For most women, the instinctual urge to clean and prepare everything for a newborn baby kicks in closer to the due date. For me, preparing for baby number three was a little easier than it was as a first-time mom getting ready for twins; however, the nudge to nest was no different. While Instagram stalked me like a hawk and tormented me with the cutest outfits and toys that the baby would only wear or play with for one day, if at all, I knew what essentials I needed and what were luxury items for my youngest. Nevertheless, getting physically prepared by changing the environment in the house, car, etc., helped to mentally prepare me for the arrival of a new member of the family.

The term nesting is actually a psychological term that is defined for when one changes their surroundings to make them feel more secure.

BOARDROOM

As you *nested* to mentally prepare and feel secure in welcoming the baby home for the first time, you can exercise the same practice in your career. If you're seeking a new role in your current organization or looking to make a move to a new company, the best way to level up is to change your environment and own your space before moving into the corner office or accepting the gavel.

- Change up your wardrobe to reflect the powerful woman you'd admire.

- Spruce up your suitcase, backpack or purse so you consistently have an accessory that screams professionalism.

- Lock down a few go-to hair or makeup looks that are easy to achieve and allow you to be comfortable and presentable at all times.

- Mentally, these tips will help you feel more prepared to network when the opportunity presents itself, or more confident in last-minute chances to speak up or ask a question in a crowded room.

Nesting in your career will help you feel more secure about making bold moves sooner than you planned. In your career, you may not have the same instinctual clock counting down to the due date, but leaning into the psychology of nesting, as you did as a new mom, and applying it to your professional life will help you boss up in no time.

Lesson 3

Information Overload—*Quality versus Quantity*

Baby's Room

In preparing to deliver twins as a first-time mom, I definitely was in unchartered territory. Not only did I not know what to expect, but many of my family and friends could not relate to having a multiple birth and couldn't offer advice on taking care of two newborns at the same time. So I turned to the next best things—books and blogs. However, that journey led me down a black hole of information, mostly negative, about what to expect. I read in horror just about every day for weeks and learned of everything that could go wrong. When I read that there was a chance the twins could be conjoined and share one body for the rest of their lives, I tapped out and took myself out of my own misery. Once I realized that there is such a thing as information overload, I relinquished the desire to read everything and leaned on trusted sources, like my OB, for positive information about moms of multiples.

Information overload is indeed a thing. And if you're not careful, you can consume tons of toxic information that can get you off track. The same tenets can apply to your career when you're thinking about transitioning to a new company or role.

BOARDROOM

Lean on similar resources when it comes to your profession, just as you did as a new mommy. Surround yourself with like-minded women who have similar ambitions, or with sources that are tailored for how you want to progress in your role. Avoid taking in all of the information about what could go wrong. Instead, digest information from experts who share positive information about taking the next step in your career.

This goes for the people around you too. If you are looking to boss up and you are greeted by discouragement and doubt from your friends or family, start keeping some of your more ambitious plans to yourself until you can identify people who will encourage your ambition and motivate you to take action.

Knowledge is power, but too much negative information can leave you stuck, with little fuel to move forward.

Lesson 4

Force-Feed —Only Take In What You Can Digest

Baby's Room

Baby number three was a good eater with a healthy appetite. He came out of the womb smacking his lips and mouth wide open, ready for milk. And while breastfeeding was going well, when I returned to work, I needed to supplement with formula. Now, for all the mamas out there who had to decide which formulas to try on their precious babies, you know the pain of this decision and how nerveracking it can be if your baby is allergic or doesn't like certain types of formula.

Overall, a well-fitting formula is crucial if you want a happy baby who will sleep. Unfortunately, one way to find that the baby doesn't like a certain formula is by the frequency of spit-ups. We were able to determine what our baby liked, and how much milk was enough, based on the amount and frequency of the spit-ups. And despite what we read or heard from the pediatrician, we soon learned you can't force-feed a baby. Naturally, the baby will show you what he likes and how much.

BOARDROOM

The same can apply to your career. Think about this when an idea about a project or initiative just isn't landing at work. One size does not fit all; sometimes adjusting the taste level makes it easier to digest.

Often we take on roles, projects, or assignments because we feel forced or pressured. And while there is nothing wrong with pushing yourself out of your comfort zone, it's important to take on aspects of work that are suitable for your skill set and expertise level so that you are allowed to thrive instead of ending up with an upset stomach, no sleep, and spit-up.

Practice writing down what you love most about your job, what aspects of your job need improvement, or what will help you gain the exposure or experience needed to transition into your next role. If an assignment or new project doesn't align with these written priorities, be honest, and do not take on the work. This is boss behavior; it will allow room for the most nourishing work that will leave you fulfilled and ready for the challenges that suit you best.

Lesson 5

Assess the Blame —*It's Not Always Someone's Fault*

Baby's Room

Late one night when I was nine months pregnant with my youngest, my husband came home after attending basketball practice with our older son. I wondered about their tardiness in getting home, but figured a late-night snack or convo with the other dads was the reason. When my husband walked into the house, he was limping. He confessed that he had attempted to make a Michael Jordanesque dunk at practice to impress the other dads; thus, he blew out his knee. More technically speaking, he tore his patellar tendon.

Needless to say, I was ready to kill my beloved husband. While I thought I might spend the last few weeks of my pregnancy with my feet elevated, eating good snacks and binge-watching television, I knew I'd have to assist with his recovery and coordinate how the older kids got to their practices and activities. Post knee surgery, I was angry. My husband got the blame for any- and everything that did not go according to plan. And I was growing more resentful by the day. I felt it was his fault; he had interrupted the plan and vision I had for the pregnancy, labor, and delivery.

What took me a while to realize is that I was missing some of the most beautiful moments with my newborn baby because I was mad at my husband. I also was missing the things to be thankful for, such as a healthy pregnancy, our nearby family support, and the ability to have all of our needs met. This went on until I had a real honest discussion with myself. The accident my husband had was just that, an accident, and this unfortunate situation would not get any better as long as I was determined to assess blame for the number of challenges we experienced during this time.

This is my most recent example of misplaced blame when there should not have been a need to assess blame at all. Can you relate? When sleep deprivation is present, your partner is usually the number one source of blame, especially during those early infant months. But you find out over time that everything is not always your partner's fault, or anyone's fault. It's just the present reality.

BOARDROOM

Think about the times at work when you're eager to place the blame on someone for a mishap or misstep. Assess the environment, and come together to find solutions, rather than pinning the blame on a particular person. This strategy will help you sleep easier at night because this happens all the time in our lives and in our careers.

When someone at our job doesn't give us the raise or the promotion we want, overloads us with work, gossips in the office, or sucks up to the person we don't get along with, we blame that person for our experiences or successes and failures at work. The reality is that, sometimes, things just happen, and our need to attribute blame to someone gets in the way of real success. Instead of getting caught up in whose fault it is that you aren't where you want to be in your professional life, channel that energy into taking action for the things you can control—such as your own professional development and how you respond to change in the workplace—and identify what professional activities fulfill you the most. Focus less on blaming others; focus more on gratitude, what you have the ability to influence, and projects that can be self-started.

Lesson 6

Unsolicited Advice —Not All Advice Is Good Advice

Baby's Room

Remember the great advice you took from a person with no kids, the one who told you how to best navigate through pregnancy, or from the stranger in the grocery store who told you how to discipline your kids? Of course not.

To all the mamas far and wide across the globe, I know that you can relate to this tip. We talked about instinct earlier, and regardless of your level of experience as a mom, you will have a certain approach to how you raise your child. However, that unique, individual, and personal aspect of parenting will not stop others from giving you advice. It will not stop well-meaning women with tons of helpful tips, men with kids, people without kids, strangers, or even other little kids from giving you parenting advice. You will get advice from everywhere, and while some snippets of advice will be welcomed, much of it will be unsolicited and unwanted.

The question is, how will you respond? A rookie mistake is to let all the advice impact you in a destructive way, to the point that it makes you feel negatively about your parenting. However, that's easier said than done. It's important to surround yourself with people in your village whom you love and trust to raise your child, ones who can uplift and encourage you and your child. Also connect often with parents whom you admire, whom you'd like to emulate, or whom you wouldn't mind influencing your child.

BOARDROOM

Remember this in your career as well. Don't take advice about your profession and career goals from people who don't understand what you do or how to best accomplish your goals, especially when you are thinking about making a new move or transition that has the potential for an increase in pay or promotion. You will receive unsolicited advice from any- and everyone. But not all advice is good advice.

The opportunity for upward mobility can create some feelings of envy, particularly in the workplace. So be thoughtful about with whom you share your ambitions and plans. People close to you may love you dearly, but they may not quite understand what you do or why you do it, and their fear of your failure may cause them to be more discouraging than encouraging. Guard how much specific guidance you receive from people who don't understand your work dynamics.

Finally, surround yourself with like-minded people who understand your field, can help you strategize to get to the next step, and will encourage you to take calculated risks. Most of all, give yourself encouraging advice to keep going, to cross the starting line on set goals, and to celebrate small wins. Don't let a pause in progress stop you from continuing the journey.

Lesson 7

Live in the Moment
—The Days Are Long,
but the Years Are Short

Baby's Room

As the saying goes, the days are long, but the years are short when raising children. I might argue that it often feels as if both the days and years are long. Despite the ever-changing ration of good to bad days, every mom finds herself asking the coveted question about her kiddos. "Where did the time go?" When you see how they've physically and emotionally grown over the years, and the many things they've accomplished, it's hard not to regret the times you did a little too much multitasking or didn't quite embrace a stage in their lives because you were antici-pating getting to the next stage.

BOARDROOM

The same can apply to your career. Embracing the current state of your career may teach you things necessary for the next chapter in your life. Don't miss the lesson because you were too busy anticipating the next moment. Your career is similar to your life; things naturally change over time. Whether you find yourself in the same role for a while or dealing with lots of exterior changes beyond your control, try to embrace the current state and learn the lessons from that moment. You may find that there are opportunities to prepare yourself for your next chapter.

By learning to be okay with your current state in your position, your anxiety or stress about what is next may be greatly reduced. When you find yourself living in the moment and enjoying the current space you're in, you may find that your focus, attention to detail, and gratitude increases.

Lesson 8

Baby-Book Memories —Document Your Progress

Baby's Room

Do you remember getting a baby book before your firstborn arrived? The one with all of the inserts and sections to document your baby's footprint, save the hospital bracelet, and record the first word and first step? And if you are anything like me, you stopped documenting so frequently as soon as the baby became mobile. And the second or third kid probably got the bare minimum insertions in the book, if they had one at all. Whether you were diligent or not, old-school or new age with your technology, every mom always tries their best to document the progress of their child. Because things change so quickly and it's great to walk down memory lane. There is also something quite healing and cathartic about writing things down, stamping a memory in time.

BOARDROOM

The same can hold true for your career. If your job requires that you complete a written evaluation every year, you are in luck. This is a great tool not only to demonstrate to your supervisor what progress you have made throughout the year, an opportunity for a raise or promotion, but to prove to yourself just how much you accomplished in one year.

Sometimes these evaluation periods can feel more like a heavy burden than an opportunity to reflect. Imagine if you waited all year to document your baby's progress. It would never get done. Just as you did with the baby book, at least for your firstborn, make a concerted effort to document your progress at work throughout the year. Keep a running document in a file and notate whenever you feel particularly accomplished and take a great sigh of relief after overcoming a challenge.

Little things add up to big accomplishments when told in a light that helps you see the full picture of who you are at work. Make note of each milestone at work; you may surprise yourself with how the little moments combined into major moves of the year.

Lesson 9

Terrible Twos
—Have a Good Cry; Then Move On

Baby's Room

Toddlers do a lot of crying. Their cries as a toddler are different, however, than their primal cries as infants when they needed one of three things—to be fed, to be changed, or to be put to sleep.

Toddlers have another set of criteria that warrant crying and often tantrums. As a mom, you know when something is wrong, when something needs immediate or medical attention, or when your baby just needs to cry out of frustration from not being able to effectively communicate to be understood.

What do you do in those situations? You let them cry it out, and then you distract them with something else. The next thing you know, the meltdown literally melts away, and we have all effectively moved on. Now, granted, some waiting periods take longer than others. But, nevertheless, the crying always stops, and the baby always moves on.

BOARDROOM

There will be times in your career when you just need to cry. Like a toddler, you may not be able to effectively communicate why you feel the need to cry. You may be frustrated with a current situation or unable to understand why an issue is happening at work.

I am giving you permission at this moment to cry. Let it out; scream into a pillow; do whatever is needed to let out that negative energy. But you must move on, and you should do it quickly. Just as no one ever said raising kids would be easy, the hiring manager could not promise you that every day would be good. However, the sooner you learn to leave the emotional outbursts behind and move on to the job at hand, the better position you will be in to make clear and rational decisions.

When your baby is having a tantrum, they can be a danger to others and themselves because the emotions make them irrational. But with some distraction, they move on, come to their senses, and commence functioning in a way that is manageable. In your career, you may have to hold yourself accountable when you are having tantrums, or solicit a trust partner to check you when you do—with an understanding that no good decisions can come from a place of extreme and irrational emotion.

Do your best to give yourself the grace to feel the frustration, let it out, and move on. Your next chapter could be the best chapter because of your ability to move on from the toddler stage to a more grown-up stage in your career.

Lesson 10

Baby Steps
—One Step at a Time

Baby's Room

The twins took their first steps at about thirteen months. Much to my chagrin, as I was hoping that they would wow their guests by walking around for their elaborate, over-the-top first birthday party; plus, many of their baby peers were walking at twelve months. During that time, I remember being so hyper-focused on their walking that I almost missed the enjoyment of their turning one and remembering the amazing year we had.

When baby number three was born, I wasn't quite thinking about his walking. In fact, I was really enjoying the crawling stage and tried to savor all of his discovery of the world at ground level. Much to my surprise, he took his first steps at ten months and was nearly running around during his first birthday party.

BOARDROOM

Sometimes we want to rush things in our career; we want to make something happen even if we aren't quite ready. Or we compare ourselves to others who have a similar resume or background, feeling deficient if we haven't reached the same level of success.

Like toddlers who transition from crawling, to walking, to running, and eventually to climbing, it's important that we understand that there are stages of achievement. Most of us have to crawl before we climb. Even when we take bias and discrimination against women and moms in the workplace out of the equation, many of us must understand that success doesn't happen overnight. In addition to taking baby steps to get to our desired career destination, we must remind ourselves that success is different for everyone. My timeline and pathway may be different from another woman's, just as my kids had different walking and milestone journeys.

Be patient with yourself when walking on the path and climbing the ladder to success. Just continue to take baby steps in the direction you want to go, and, like proud parents, make sure that, around you, there's a team of people cheering you on every step of the way.

Lesson 11

Use Your Words —*Your Voice Matters*

Baby Steps

For those moms who can fondly remember the toddler stages, you might attest to not the terrible twos but the terrible threes. That age where ability, limitations, and comprehension intersect in a perfect way, similar to a car crash. Three-year-olds can, and want to, do many things that they could not do when they were one or two, yet they still need a lot of assistance. Thus, the tantrums enter at these very moments.

I remember telling the twins many times to use their words when the onset of a tantrum was getting out of hand and a full-on meltdown was in sight. I knew that they had the capability to articulate what they wanted, but I soon realized that they did not realize that they could. The moments of calming them down came with a lot of encouragement to help them understand that their words could be more effective than screaming and crying.

BOARDROOM

In our careers, we sometimes have tantrums of our own. We get frustrated with our bosses and coworkers for not understanding our wants and needs, particularly when we haven't communicated them. I mean, they should just know, right!? They've worked with us long enough!

The reality is that you do, in fact, have to use your words, past the age of three, to get what you want and need in life. Your boss and coworkers cannot make assumptions about what you need. Much of your frustration may come from a place in which you think you don't have a voice, or you don't know how to use it.

Work on speaking up for yourself and empowering people around you to do the same. You will progress in your career and attain leadership opportunities simply because you mastered what we all strived to teach our toddlers during the terrible twos and threes.

Lesson 12

Short Memory —Forgetfulness Is a Source of Freedom

Baby's Room

Park and playground time was always interesting to me. Honestly, not my favorite activity, although I knew it was great for the kids' development and socialization. There were always too many opportunities for accidents, germs, and the occasional run-in with another child over swing and slide time.

I'll never forget those short-lived squabbles on the playground. From steps away, I would hear "Mommy" being called out, followed by "He's not my friend." I would provide comfort for a few minutes, and, the next thing I knew, my kid was proceeding to play with the same child whom they had just unfriended moments ago.

After a short chuckle, I always wondered why adults couldn't play as nicely or manage to have as short a memory as the kids.

BOARDROOM

Throughout my career, I've had plenty of moments where I felt wronged, betrayed, or treated unfairly. But I learned that, over time, it benefited me personally and professionally to have a short memory. When I held grudges for a long time in the workplace, it always made me so uncomfortable as I attempted to

avoid the person in the hallway or not sit with them at the team meetings.

But when I forgot about small grievances sooner, I felt lighter and like the bigger person. Ultimately, not taking things personally allowed me to be more professional and achieve the task at hand.

When I ran for office the first time, I ran against what some would consider the establishment; I was the underdog with little name recognition and no start-up money. A couple who owned a business in the city offered to host my first fundraiser at their shop, which would have sent a great message to small business owners, long-standing community members, etc. However, just days before the fundraiser, the couple canceled the event in fear that they would upset my opponents.

I was left scrambling for a place to host my first event, which could in many ways set the tone of my entire campaign. All's well that ends well, and I was able to have a successful fundraiser, even without the couple who canceled on me. Shortly thereafter, I was admittedly upset, but decided to have a short memory. I decided that, if and when I would see them again, I would be kind and gracious, ask about their family, and not bring up the event.

Months after I won the election, I ran into them in the grocery store, and they looked as if they wanted to turn around and go to the next aisle. But we approached each other, made small talk, and moved on. I could see that they were visibly surprised by my warm demeanor, and I walked away with my head held high. That moment reminded me that some people may unintentionally or intentionally create barriers in your career, but if you don't let those barriers stop you, you are the true winner.

From that day forth, I committed to having a short memory, just like my kids on the playground, as often as possible. That approach increased my professional possibilities and strengthened my confidence.

Lesson 13

Pooh-pooh Belongs in the Potty—*Leave Your Smelly Mess at Home*

Baby's Room

The days of potty training were oh-so fun, said no mom ever. I required next level patience when potty training the twins, and some of my sanity I may never gain back. It, by far, was one of the hardest stages of their childhood to get through. I tried just about every trick and tip that I could learn, including one that allowed the twins to walk around diaper-free. But that freedom came at a cost, as I discovered that one of them was going "number two" in select corners of the house. What fun! In addition to trying to wrangle each of them into the bathroom, I had to be on the search for pockets of poop throughout the house. Once my frustration reached a breaking point, which didn't take long, I had to have a meeting with the twins and clearly explain that "Pooh-pooh goes in the potty!"

BOARDROOM

Just as toddlers feel a sense of freedom walking around the house diaper-free, we often get a little too comfortable at work. I mean, it's totally natural, as sometimes we spend more time with the people at work than we do with our families. Therefore, we often share a lot of personal information with our coworkers. And while that creates bonding moments and connections, there is just some information you should not share at work.

What happens when you share with your coworkers too much about a bad relationship or about the way you handle conflict with your siblings, and then you are up for a promotion? What will those coworkers say about your ability to make sound decisions or your ability to resolve conflict?

While most can differentiate your personal self from your work self, true leaders show up authentically to work; thus, they don't have different personas at work than they do in the world. Therefore, do your best to leave the bad and ugly at home—essentially, leave the pooh-pooh in the potty and continue to bring the good, positive, and productive to the office.

Lesson 14

Play with Dirt—Getting Your Hands Dirty Is a Lesson

Baby's Room

Like many moms, as a new mom, I was obsessed with keeping my babies' hands clean. I found myself hand sanitizing and wiping them down after every adult squeezed their chubby fingers, when they touched any railing, or when they fell on the ground after wobbling across the playground. And then baby number three came with a new set of world problems, being born into a global pandemic that put a new spin on the concept of germs and sanitation.

Regardless of my determination to keep all of my kiddos' hands clean to prevent illness, their hands, no doubt, were often dirty and exposed to countless germs. And as most moms know and understand over time, playing with actual dirt and sand are learning opportunities for our kids. Many of us who confess to helicopter-parent tendencies have to come to grips with not being able to be with our kids all of the time. We must also understand that in those moments in which we cannot operate as a safety net for our kids are the exact moments we want our kids to use critical thinking, reasoning, negotiation, and problem solving. But how can they do that if we never allow them to get their hands dirty, fall, or fail?

BOARDROOM

The same applies to your ability to develop in your career. When you consistently play it safe at work and don't participate in activities to "get your hands dirty" or do things that are hard or even below your pay grade, you miss an opportunity to learn something outside of your wheelhouse and grow professionally.

Additionally, if you manage others, try to participate in activities that you usually are in charge of directing. It is an opportunity to demonstrate servant leadership by participating in activities that are seemingly beneath you. If you want to authentically be a boss, then it's vital that you learn every aspect of your organization—from the janitorial roles to those of the CEO.

Like our kiddos, the best way to learn is by doing. And doing things that are hard, tedious, and sometimes dirty yields the most learnable lessons.

Lesson 15

Fitting In—
Assess Whether an
Environment Is the
Right Fit for You

Baby's Room

One March when the twins were about seven or eight years old, I recall my dad asking about whether the kids had enough green to wear to school in preparation for Saint Patrick's Day. He called the night before and the morning of. At first, I thought it was cute that he cared so much, but those same thoughts turned into concern as my dad pressed me about their wardrobe. He later disclosed to me that when he was their age or younger, he had a tough memory about not wearing green to school and being pinched throughout the day by his classmates. Today, we would call that harassment or bullying. But during my dad's school-aged days, it was just a part of the culture. Nevertheless, the pinching, probing, and taunting had a lasting impact on him, and understandably so.

His story got me thinking about who made up this tradition. Moreover, who allowed it to spill over to the schoolhouse? When I think about the premise behind the tradition, essentially the message is that if you don't fit in by wearing green, you deserve to be called out and in a physical manner. Thankfully, as a community, I think we've made headway on distancing ourselves from such traditions, but the fact that this type of activity went on so long in our culture calls for a pause of reflection at the very least.

BOARDROOM

Just as the pinching and taunting spree that often happened in schools for Saint Patrick's Day, some traditions in the workplace have stuck around, and they have had a lasting impact, even though they are not right, appropriate, or supportive of a healthy work environment. Think about who sits with whom in a conference room, who attends work parties or events outside of the office. Unconsciously, we may be signaling to coworkers that they do not fit in, and that message may have a lasting impact.

If you feel out of place at work because of unspoken rules or office culture, don't rush to "wear green" if it's not authentically something you would do. Who knows, to demonstrate true leadership, your role may be to change the culture in the workplace. On the contrary, this environment may be a clue to you that you may not be able to thrive in such an environment and that it's time to move on. Either way, focus more on doing a great job, rather than on fitting in, especially if the methods of fitting in are not rooted in a supportive and inclusive culture.

Lesson 16

Most Popular— Teach People How to Treat You

Baby's Room

When the twins were around ten, I started to notice a real difference in the way that they cultivated and maintained friendships. My son collected friends, so to speak. He had a big group of friends that only seemed to get bigger and closer every year. My daughter, on the other hand, routinely had one to two good friends, and these friends were replaced easily. My son was forgiving of flaws, transgressions, etc. I imagine that's how he kept such a large group of friends for a long time. My daughter, however, was much more selective, and one sign of wrongdoing, even if it wasn't directed at her, and that friend was on the chopping block.

I definitely related more to my son, as I was that way in school. I didn't meet many people I didn't call a friend, and now that I think about it, this probably contributed to my success in winning homecoming queen and senior class president in high school (shameless back-in-the-day plug!). For a while, I didn't understand how my daughter's friends were so dispensable, but after a while I realized that she was, at a young age, already very clear about how she wanted to be treated by others, particularly her friends. My son was focused more on quantity, while my daughter was concerned about quality.

BOARDROOM

When being popular is important, and when you desire to be liked in the workplace, it's difficult to be an authentic leader because it's impossible to please everyone all of the time. And once others find out that you are a people pleaser, willing to do what they want to gain their approval, the chances of being taken advantage of exponentially increase.

When serving in political office, I experienced high highs and low lows in terms of popularity amongst my constituents. Tempting it was to experience the high highs over and over again by responding to all of the requests of the loud, but many times minority, voices. I had to take a lesson out of my daughter's book and align myself with colleagues and constituents who matched my values and vision for the city, rather than make decisions based on my desire to be liked. What I gained from being more selective about the people and issues that I associated myself with was an opportunity to lead from an incredibly authentic and genuine place. This transparency has resulted in more opportunities to lead, even outside of elected office.

Lesson **17**

Couch Superman —Fear of Failure Can Cause You to Fall Instead of Fly

Baby's Room

When my son was about six years old, he used to give me a heart attack when attempting to do crazy things around the house, including thinking that he was Superman or Spiderman and attempting to fly (via jumping) off the couch, stairs, or any highish place in the house. Nine times out of ten, he fell with close calls, nearly breaking or spraining something. But he never seriously hurt himself, and after a while, he learned how to fall by rolling or tucking, etc. I soon came to grips with the fact that this type of behavior would not stop as long as I allowed him to see Marvel movies. I eventually stopped having near strokes and began to admire his lack of fear.

BOARDROOM

Imagine what we could do if we operated without fear. If we weren't afraid to fall. Like my son, we might figure out over time, not to avoid the fall, but to do it better and safer. This is what most of us call calculated risks. Women are very good at analyzing the risk before leaping. Often, this works in our favor because we avoid making decisions that could be harmful to us or our families. I would argue that we are much better at this than our husbands, sons, and dads. However, this strength can often be our weakness when taking on leadership roles at work or in the community. We often let the fear of the risks outweigh the opportunities and the potential rewards.

Running for office for the first time was risky, no doubt. I prepped for years to launch a campaign in what I thought would be a fairly benign political environment. I thought I calculated every obstacle. But once I was knee-deep in the campaign, some of the obstacles were unforeseen. However, once the campaign started, I was already leaping midair, and there was no turning back. I had to prepare for the landing, rather than abandon the mission.

In the end, my decision to take a risk and run for office led to a political win and a fulfilling political career. I often think back to that time when I approach a decision about an opportunity that has a lot of unforeseen obstacles. I think about how sometimes you just have to jump and brace yourself for a fall or failure. Just as my son jumped off the couch, the more you take those leaps of faith, the better you get at falling, and often in your career, the more you take leaps, the greater your chances are of flying.

Lesson 18

Cool Kids' Table —You Don't Fit In because You Were Born to Stand Out

Baby's Room

During after-school car rides home, my daughter frequently referenced the "cool kids," a group of popular girls at her school. It kind of broke my heart in a way to hear her talk about them as though these kids were above her or out of her league.

But one day she came home excited that she was invited to sit at the cool kids' table. However, that excitement soon dwindled as she learned that the cool kids were not as cool as she thought. They spent the majority of their lunch period talking about boys, gossiping about other girls, and bragging about goofing off in class.

For my studious daughter, this type of behavior was so far from being cool, and although she was excited to have been invited to eat lunch with them, she found comfort in knowing that maybe she wasn't invited earlier to the table because she wasn't boy crazy, didn't find it funny to talk about others, and loved getting good grades.

She continued to be friendly and say hi in the future, but she walked with a little more confidence, knowing that she was just as cool, if not more so, than the kids at the cool kids' table.

BOARDROOM

How many of us can relate to what my daughter went through in middle school? And how many of us are still longing to sit at the "cool kids' table" in our careers. The real question is, how do we work through that need to be accepted or invited? Instead of dwelling on the imposter syndrome, it's crucial that we own the space we're in and find a way to present our experiences and perspectives as unique assets to our leadership and management styles.

I have found myself in the space of a middle schooler far too many times as a grown woman. Longing to be included and accepted, and letting imposter syndrome and fear weigh me down in a way that makes it hard to move forward. When I found encouragement to move past those feelings and demanded or made space for myself at the table, I found that those same people whom I was intimidated by or longed to be accepted by were not necessarily smarter or more talented than I was. They simply were more comfortable in the space, having been there longer or having blended in well because they looked like everyone else at the table.

Think about that the next time you want a seat at a certain table, and ask yourself why. Or when you get a seat, be sure to value what you bring to the table, and do not feel intimidated about making meaningful contributions or asking difficult questions. I can almost guarantee that you will find that the people around the table are not as intimidating as you thought and that you have just as much to offer. You will also find that you are pretty cool in your own right. Not only do you deserve a seat at the cool table, but also you have the ability to create your own.

Lesson 19

When I Grow Up —Giving Yourself Permission to Have Big and Aspirational Goals

Baby's Room

When my oldest son was about eight years old, he used to love going to Medieval Times. He participated in all of the antics, from cheering for our assigned knight, to the barbaric eating, to adoring the princess who received the coveted rose. He loved it all. So much so that after one visit, he asked to purchase a Knight in Training video that was available in the gift shop...for the low price of $24.99!

I purchased the video without a lot of thought, but, months later, I found that he had watched the video dozens of times. Therefore, I shouldn't have been surprised when he came running to me one day and professed that he knew what he wanted to be when he grew up.

"Mommy, Mommy, I know what I want to be when I grow up," he shouted. "I want to be a knight at Medieval Times!"

I quickly responded that knights in the way that he saw them perform at Medieval Times were not real, and it was just a show that people put on for entertainment. His swift retort was that he could then one day aspire to be one of those performers. I shot that down, firing back that he would not make a lot of money doing that for a living and that he should think about becoming an engineer or a doctor.

The look on my son's face after my response was devastating, and I realized in that moment that I had made a big mistake—I crashed the flight of a dream before it even grew wings. And I regretted that moment for a long time because I had sent a strong message to him that we aren't allowed to have unique and personal dreams that don't fit the standard of society.

BOARDROOM

I'm sure you can relate to this story. You can probably very easily think of a time when a dream of yours was killed, or when you unconsciously killed the dreams of others. Far too often, as adults, we project our fears onto others. If we are uncertain about something, we discourage each other from pursuing the unknown. Or if we have previous experience, but it's negative, albeit out of love and concern, we caution others from taking that same path.

In my career, there have been many instances in which I talked about pursuing a promotion or a change and was met with nothing but discouragement, usually from family and friends closest to me. The best ways to change these responses were to (1) be judicious with whom I share my big dreams, and (2) work on creating a circle of people in my life whom I can trust to provide wise but positive counsel.

This experience also fueled me to be better to the people sharing their dreams with me, particularly women. I allowed them a space to just dream. To talk out the logistics, pros, and cons before offering any critical feedback. Most times, I encouraged self-reflection and introspection that would allow them to do what felt best to them.

As a result, I have taken on some big challenges and jobs professionally because I had people in my life who supported my willingness to dream big. Additionally, I have helped propel many women into high spaces in their careers, in part, because of my encouragement.

Although it was unfortunate that I veered my son away from a career as a knight, I learned a valuable lesson after he shared his dream with me. I learned to be a better listener and to allow him, others around me, and myself to dream big and to do it in a daring way!

Lesson 20

Spread Your Wings— Expand Your Horizons to Expose Yourself to What Is Possible

Baby's Room

I grew up in a two-parent household in which both parents worked. I was the oldest of four, and in many ways, I had always thought of my upbringing as being akin to an average Black-American, middle-class family. It wasn't until I became an adult and had more in-depth conversations with my parents that I began to really understand that the average lifestyle I enjoyed was not accomplished without some real sacrifices on the part of my parents.

One part of my childhood that always stood out for me was our family vacations. From interesting trips to Alaska, to family reunions in Louisiana, to weeks at a resort in Mexico, my parents always ensured that we would fly somewhere as a family. And although I understood that two adults plus four kids was no small expense, it was something my parents thought was important to splurge on.

What I learned to appreciate as an adult was how my parents made those annual trips a reality. My dad worked as a terminal agent for Alaska Airlines for years, working at night after working a nine-to-five job as a computer scientist. That's right—he would take off a suit and tie to put on a uniform to perform a physically intensive job, night after night, so that he could take advantage of the flight benefits. Additionally, my mom had to sacrifice by handling dinner, homework, and bath time for all four kids, by herself, while my dad worked nights and after she had worked all day as well. Because of their sacrifices, we went on trips from Alaska to Africa, and my siblings and I were exposed to travel and the world, made possible by a road less traveled.

BOARDROOM

I often think about this creative yet taxing decision my parents made to expose my siblings and me to more opportunities. In today's culture, where social media rules, it's easy to compare ourselves to each other based on the end product. Rarely do we see the journey that led to a promotion, a job move, or even something like a speaking engagement or published article.

Like my parents, you can get creative when attempting to get the additional exposure needed for more opportunities at work. There is not one path for getting your message out there, working on your brand, or solidifying yourself as an expert in your field. Put your ego aside, and be okay with the methods that may not be Instagrammable, but are still effective in getting you the position you want. You may have to put in some ground-level work—such as sitting on committees, volunteering in the community, or donating your expertise to a good cause. Consider all of these activities the exposure and experience that will set you up for your next trip and life chapter.

Lesson 21

Do as I Say—Practice What You Preach Because You Never Know Who Is Watching

Baby's Room

We've all heard that saying, "Do as I say, not as I do," from adults growing up. You may even be guilty of using that line once or twice with your kiddos. While a little anti-quated, I certainly understand why this saying was once popular. As moms, we know all too well that our kiddos are parrots and mimes and will emulate us exactly, regardless of what we say.

I love the quote by James Baldwin that says, "Children have never been very good at listening to their elders, but they have never failed to imitate them."

When my daughter was in kindergarten, she was in a class in which the teacher gave out green, yellow, and red apples every day after school to reflect what kind of day each child had—green meant good; yellow, concerning; and red, bad. I always thought the rubric was strange, as red apples are sweet, and green apples are sour. Nevertheless, my daughter routinely came home with a green-apple card, until one day when she walked up to me after school with a tear-stained face and a red-apple card in her hand.

I asked her and the teacher what happened, and the teacher proceeded to tell me that my daughter received a red apple because she licked her friend on the face. I repeated her statement to get clarity. "She licked her face?" I asked. But before the teacher could get much of the explanation out, I profusely apologized and walked away, embarrassed, *shocked, and confused. I reserved the inquisition for the car, in which I asked my daughter to explain exactly why she would do this, and to her friend, no less.*

My daughter proceeded to explain that she thought it was a fun game that people played with others whom they liked, just as my sister (her aunt) played a game with her (apparently when I wasn't home) in which they chased each other with the threat of stinky spit or a lick. Although this sounded gross and not fun at all, I at least understood where such an idea originated.

This incident solidified for me that kids are indeed sponges who pick up on things that we don't even realize.

BOARDROOM

At work, do you lead by example? Are you the change you want to see in the office or in the community?

Over the last ten years, I have coincidentally employed women support staff who have gotten pregnant and requested maternity leave. As someone who has not always been happy with the way I was treated when announcing my pregnancy, or during maternity leave, I always made a concerted effort to be supportive in a way that showed that I placed value on my staff as women and mothers, first, over their importance to me as employees. I encouraged them to take the time needed to learn about all their covered benefits and to take advantage of additional time, breaks, or accommodations they could use once they returned to the office. As a mom who knew how hard it was to be pregnant while working a demanding job, I was adamant about creating a different space for the women who worked for me. Even today, I continue to hear from these same women about how thankful they were to have a boss, like me, who was understanding during such a big transition in their lives.

This example reminded me that I had the power to influence change in the workplace, and although I may not have experienced the benefits directly, I was able to contribute to a holistic change in the office, establishing work-from-home policies and breast-pumping areas in the office.

Lesson 22

Participation Trophies—Celebrate Small Wins and Cultivate the Art of Showing Up

Baby's Room

When the twins were starting to play sports, it was almost comical to see how big and ornate the trophies were at the end of the season. Regardless of the shots scored, games won, or tournaments played, every member of the team received a trophy. Although my husband (the übercompetitive former college-football player) would disagree with me, I always appreciated the participation trophies at the end of the season. I understood the concept that the trophy could represent different things to different kids. The trophy marked the end of trying something new, working with a team, or accomplishing a personal record. A trophy for every member of the team also signified that on a team, everyone brings something unique to the team and is deserving of recognition.

BOARDROOM

Like the Little League, Pop Warner, and AYSO (American Youth Soccer Organization) days, being a working mom can sometimes feel like a contact sport. We are working to juggle family and work, and to ultimately succeed at home and in our careers. It's not easy—no one ever said it would be.

But it can be a little easier and a little more manageable if we pause to reflect on the lessons that we learned as we watched our kiddos grow into people we are proud of. If we apply those lessons to our work, we will watch our careers grow and develop into something we can equally be proud of.

And just as the players with the most or least game time who received a trophy at the end of the season, give yourself a pat on the back for doing a great job at both mothering and working. You deserve a participation trophy because you are participating, showing up, engaging, and learning to thrive, versus survive, as a mom and a boss.

Lesson 23

Growing Pains—
Change Is Hard,
but It Stretches You

Baby's Room

My daughter had an early growth spurt, shooting past her twin brother at about age ten; she continued to grow through fifteen years of age, until he finally caught up to her. She used to complain about the pains in her knees and back—similar to the pains my grandmother would gripe about. So much so that one day I asked Granny what she did to relieve her aches and pains; I wanted to use her methods to relieve my daughter in her time of need. Granny gave me plenty of safe organic tips, one in particular worked exceptionally well.

"Place a banana peel in boiling-hot water; then serve the water as tea, or add lemon for taste, and have her drink it," she said.

Over time, the potassium offered relief from the growing pains, and the banana water was a soothing treat my daughter enjoyed before bed. The growing pains were also a soothing reminder to my daughter that she was still indeed growing. She enjoyed being one of the tallest girls in her class and definitely liked holding that leverage over her brother. Ultimately, she not only tolerated, but embraced, the growing pains, because it was a signal that something was happening in her body and that she was only changing for the better.

BOARDROOM

Similar to the growth spurts and growing pains that our children go through, we will experience growing pains in our careers. Many of us get extremely comfortable in our roles and our places of work—so much so that any change in responsibility or in operations feels like an inconvenience.

But just as my daughter changed her perspective about growing pains, we must do the same in order to grow as professionals and in our careers. We must embrace change and instances that push us out of our comfort zones, forcing us into places that require us to work with new people or learn new skills.

It's through the pain of change that we can discover more about our abilities and our capacity to adapt. In the moments of change, we can also learn about the things that provide us the most joy or purpose in our current roles, things that perhaps had been lost in a sea of complacency. Moments of change and discomfort can also help you to refine your leadership style, your values, and your professional ethics, thereby cementing what you will and won't accommodate in your career.

Lesson 24

Period Party— Shifting the Narrative through Perspective

Baby's Room

I was an early bloomer and started menstruating at around ten years of age. When my daughter was going for a regular checkup with the pediatrician, we learned that she probably would experience a similar time line, and, lo and behold, she got her period at eleven years old. Like most girls her age, she was not excited about this change in her body and the new responsibilities of having to carry pads in her backpack, avoid leakage, and endure the monthly cramps and fatigue.

When I got the call one day from school that the dreaded period had arrived, I felt so bad and didn't quite know how to help my daughter feel better about the new normal she would have to embrace. So instead of helping her throw a pity party, I planned a period party and treated the moment as a special time in her life that was demonstrative of her growing up into a young lady. Similar to growing pains, her period was a signal that she was changing and growing.

With some incentives, I encouraged her to change her perspective. When she arrived home from school, I had plenty of pad options, but also some pain-reliever medicine, herbal teas, chocolate and her favorite sour snacks, face masks, and some comfortable pajamas. I explained to her that with when that time of the month comes, if needed, she could call a time-out to take care of herself. As a family with a busy schedule, this sounded great to her. In that moment, I helped change her perspective about her menstrual period; instead of an inevitable curse, it became a welcomed change.

BOARDROOM

Throughout our careers, we will be faced with presenting new and different ideas to stakeholders who need to provide support in order for the initiative to move forward. Just as I had to change for my daughter the long-standing narrative of most women and girls about their periods, you may be faced with trying to change the narrative about a long-standing tradition or practice in the workplace.

In sectors such as government and public service, Fortune 500 companies, and male-dominated industries, the narrative about women leaders may need to change. It may be our role to help offer a new perspective, or to demonstrate a living example to prove that being a woman leader as well as a mom is an asset, not a liability. In America, there are countless examples in which women have had to compromise time with their children, or even the possibility of having children at all, in order to rise to high levels of leadership.

But we have the power to change that narrative and to demonstrate that workplace and societal expectations can benefit from embracing the assets that working mothers bring to the table. As demonstrated throughout this book, raising children provides a level of insight, introspection, and experience that allows us to be effective leaders in today's environment.

Lesson 25

Activate Mom-Boss Mode Here—Journal and Reflection Time

Let's reflect on some of the lessons you've learned as a mom, those that can translate into your entering boss mode and making moves in your career.

Remember the Time

When I was most scared as a mom.

_____

_____

_____

What did you do to push through the fear?

_____

_____

_____

What was the outcome?

_____

_____

_____

What lesson did you learn about yourself?

_____

_____

_____

What did you learn about overcoming doubt and trusting your instincts, and how can you relate it to your career?

_____

_____

_____

Remember the Time

When my kids surprised me with something they knew, or did, that I thought they weren't capable of.

_____

_____

_____

How did that make you feel?

_____

_____

_____

What did that experience teach you about their abilities?

_____

_____

_____

What lessons did you learn about overcoming limitations, either set by you or by others, that you could apply to your career?

_____

_____

_____

Envision the Future

What does your future life look like after raising kids?

_____

_____

_____

Are you working on, or involved in, a passion project? If so, describe your role.

_____

_____

_____

What is your role with your adult children? Do you engage with them hands-on daily or weekly? Or are you more hands-off, with holidays and vacations being the main quality time you spend with them?

_____

_____

_____

Moving Mountains and Eliminating Barriers

If childcare was not a barrier, what would you do with your time if someone you trust could help with caring for your children?

_____

_____

_____

If finances weren't an issue and you did not have to work, what would you do with your time?

_____

_____

_____

What are you passionate about?

_____

_____

_____

Where do you find moments of purpose?

_____

_____

_____

How do you recharge?

_____

_____

_____

When you walk into a room, what is the theme song in your head?

_____

_____

_____

Being a working mom is more than a full-time job, so, it is easy to get so caught up in our two important roles, at work and at home, that we don't take the time to reflect, envision, and dream.

After completing this reflective exercise, continue to think about ways that your kids have taught you valuable lessons about others, yourself, and the world around you. Think about how those lessons can carry over into other parts of your life—such as the way you treat yourself, view others, or apply emotional intelligence in places like your workplace or in organizations.

I promise you will find that you have already learned valuable lessons that can help you address real challenges in your professional career. Do yourself a favor, and utilize those lessons as your opportunity to level up and take your career to the next stage. If it's not a promotion or job change, at least remember how being a mom is an asset, and how it can help you lead with more confidence and greater empathy in any role you take on in life.

Remember, being a mom and a boss are synonymous. You've got this!

"A MOTHER'S LOVE LIBERATES."

Maya Angelou

"KNOWING WHAT MUST BE DONE DOES AWAY WITH FEAR."

Rosa Parks

"FOR ME, BEING A MOTHER MADE ME A BETTER PROFESSIONAL, BECAUSE COMING HOME EVERY NIGHT TO MY GIRLS REMINDED ME WHAT I WAS WORKING FOR.
AND BEING A PROFESSIONAL MADE ME A BETTER MOTHER, BECAUSE BY PURSUING MY DREAMS, I WAS MODELING FOR MY GIRLS HOW TO PURSUE THEIR DREAMS."

Michelle Obama

"THE PHRASE 'WORKING MOTHER,' IS REDUNDANT."

Jane Sellman

Letitia Clark is a former city mayor, a wife, and a mom of three—teenage twins and a toddler. She is a long-standing community leader and communications professional who has found success with her career and family.

Before reaching the age of forty, she became the first Black-female mayor of Tustin, California, and had baby number three while serving as the city's leader. Letitia is the recipient of several awards and recognition for her advocacy work on behalf of women and girls.

She is notably the author of a children's book, her debut published work, *Mommy Is the Mayor*.

Mommy is the Mayor

ISBN Hardcover: 978-1-63765-131-5

ISBN Paperback: 978-1-63765-041-7